WHAT'S for DINNER, DAD?
and other selections

S. Alan Cohen / Joan S. Hyman

The Reading House Series™
from Random House

ACKNOWLEDGMENTS

The following selections in this Reader are original material by THE READING HOUSE authors, S. Alan Cohen and Joan S. Hyman:

Selection on page 7, "Sky Writing—Dragon Style"
Selection on page 12, "Why the Elephant's Trunk Is Long"
Selections on pages 27-35, "Evil, Prince of Prefixes, and Happy King Henry" (Parts I & II)
Selections on pages 37-50, "Proud Zachary the Magnificent Zebra" (Parts I-III)
Selection on page 52, "A Balloon for Every Baboon"
Selection on page 57, "Terry Tuna's Trick"
Selection on page 62, "Sooner or Later, Sounds Make a Difference"
Selection on page 67, "How the Sea Got Its Salt" (based on a Norse legend)
Selection on page 72, "The Flying Machine"
Selection on page 77, "Up for Grabs—A Giraffe Story"
Selection on page 82, "He's Nuts About Squirrels"
Selection on page 87, "What's for Dinner, Dad?"

Grateful acknowledgment is made to the authors, publishers, agents, and individuals for their permission to use the following materials:

Selection on page 2 from THE SUN DANCE PEOPLE: THE PLAINS INDIANS THEIR PAST AND PRESENT by Richard Erdoes. Copyright © 1972 by Richard Erdoes. Reprinted by permission of Alfred A. Knopf, Inc.

Selection on page 3, "Grandfather and I" by Joseph Concha from THE WAY, edited by Shirley Hill Witt and Stan Steiner. Copyright © 1972 by Alfred A. Knopf, Inc. Reprinted by permission of Joseph Concha.

Selection on page 4, "In One Day My Mother Grew Old" by Courtney Moyah from THE WAY, edited by Shirley Hill Witt and Stan Steiner. Copyright © 1972 by Alfred A. Knopf, Inc. Reprinted by permission of Courtney Moyah.

"The Fruit Bowl" by Charles Conroy on page 17, poem by Annie Clayton on page 18, poem by Erin Harold on page 19, "Mr. TV" by Thomas Kennedy on page 20, from WISHES, LIES AND DREAMS by Kenneth Koch and The Students of P.S. 61 in New York City. Copyright © 1970 by Kenneth Koch. Reprinted by permission of Random House, Inc. and by International Creative Management.

Selections on pages 22-25 from A FEW FLIES AND I by Issa, selected by Jean Merrill and Ronni Solbert. Copyright © 1969 by Jean Merrill. Reprinted by permission of Pantheon Books, a division of Random House, Inc. and by McIntosh and Otis, Inc.

Photo Credits
Photo on page 2 by Michal Heron
Photo on page 3 by John Running/Stock, Boston
Photo on page 5 by Michal Heron
Illustrations by Publishers Graphics
Every effort has been made to trace the ownership of all copyrighted material in this book and to obtain permission for its use.

Library of Congress Cataloging in Publication Data

Cohen, S. Alan
  What's for dinner, dad? and other selections.

  (The Reading House Series from Random House : Structural analysis (red))
  SUMMARY: Eighteen reading selections which develop various basic reading skills. Follow-up activities are included.
  1. Readers—1950-   [1. Readers] I. Hyman, Joan S., joint author. II. Title.
PE1119.C5995   428'.6   76-17080
ISBN 0-394-04348-0

Copyright © 1977 by Random House, Inc.

Manufactured in the United States of America
ISBN 0-394-04348-0

6789H98765432 1

CONTENTS

For each Instructional Objective (I-O) the student masters in Tests and Tasks for
Structural Analysis (Red), there is an appropriate selection in this RH Reader. The I-O
numeral listed in the Contents directs the students to the particular reading selection
and its follow-up activities.

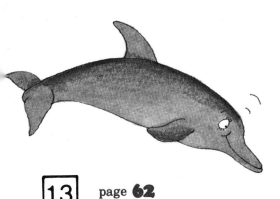

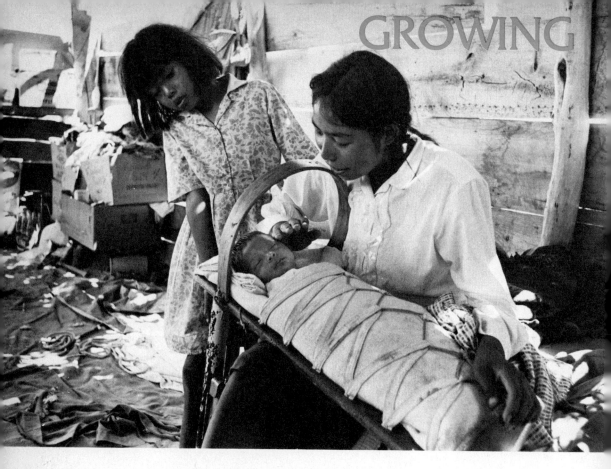

NEW LIFE
Omaha Prayer on the Birth of a Child

Ho! Sun, moon and stars,
All you that move in the
heavens, listen to me!
Into your midst
new life has come.
Make its path smooth.

Ho! Winds, clouds and rain,
you that move in the air.
Into your midst
new life has come.
Make its path smooth!

Structural Analysis ☐1   2

GRANDFATHER AND I
by Joseph Concha

Grandfather and I
talk
Grandfather sings
I dance
Grandfather teaches
I learn
Grandfather dies
I cry

I wait
patiently
to see Grandfather
in the world of darkness

I miss
my
Grandfather

Patient waiting
is weighted
by loneliness
I cry and cry and cry
When
will I see him?

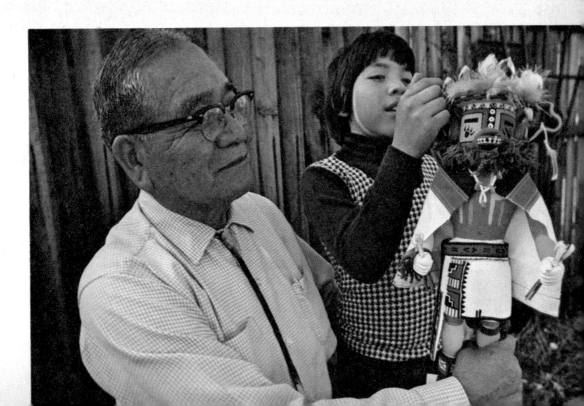

IN ONE DAY MY MOTHER GREW OLD
by Courtney Moyah

In one day my mother grew old.
I walked the trail, looking down
onto the ground. In one day
my mother grew old.

I came to the end of the trail near
the river. I stopped to listen to
the flowing water. In one day
my mother grew old.

I looked at the river. I heard
waves from a river beyond sight.
The waves wanted to say something,
but went away. In one day
my mother grew old.

I walked and looked at my mother's face.
She was quiet. She was life. She
waved as I came closer and held me in
her arms until water from the river
came to my eyes.

GROWING

(pages 2-5)

1. How does the person who wrote the second poem feel about his grandfather?

2. In the first poem, what does the poet mean by "Make its path smooth"?

3. How do you think the poet feels in the poem, "In One Day My Mother Grew Old"?

4. One poet uses the word <u>something</u>. Name three other compound words that begin with <u>some</u>.

5. What is the compound word in the second poem?

ANSWERS

SKY WRITING– DRAGON STYLE

Sir Blendalot, mighty knight of the Sound Table, stood high in his saddle as he looked down into the valley far below.

"Oh, what a happy day," said Blendalot to Drexel, his faithful dragon. "Tomorrow I will marry the lady of my dreams, Proud Priscilla, ruler of many lands."

"It's going to be a great day," said Drexel. "I can't wait to see myself in a fancy tuxedo. I'm naturally handsome, you know."

Sir Blendalot continued, "She'll be here within the hour, so there's no time to waste! Drexel, do you think you could get up a little display of fiery breath to fancy up the welcoming ceremonies?"

Drexel looked sadly at Sir Blendalot. "You know I'd really like to help you out, but I have an allergy, and my drippy nose always puts out my fire."

Not even listening to Drexel, Blendalot continued, "It would be super; twenty dancing sea horses, a cupcake maker and four pairs of candle dippers to sing songs of love. All you have to do is write her name, Proud Priscilla, in dragon flames across the night sky."

Drexel smiled happily. "I'll be a famous dragon. It's a great idea. I'll do it! Yes, I *will* do it! Just watch my smoke!"

Soon, all was ready. The crowd stood in silence, awaiting Priscilla.

"Here she comes! Priscilla is coming!" cried the village guard.

"Stand back!" yelled the street cleaner. "Proud Priscilla is coming in her golden coach!"

Sir Blendalot took a small handkerchief from his saddlebag and wiped a few spots of rust from his armor. He held his breath.

The coach came to a sudden stop. Proud Priscilla stepped from the coach.

Sir Blendalot gave the signal.

Twenty sea horses began to whirl and twirl on their tiny little tails. They danced for seven minutes without stopping for breath. Then the crowd went wild as the cupcake maker baked and iced three hundred vanilla, chocolate and strawberry cupcakes. The candle dippers began to dip their candles and sing songs of love. Priscilla remained silent.

Then came Drexel's big moment. He inhaled a great breath, warmed up his flamer and let out a mighty puff. A great flame shot from his nostrils. His dragon fire worked—no drip, no allergy, just hot dragon fire and smoke. Oh, was Drexel delighted! He puffed out the letters in rapid fire as the crowd stood in awe.

W-E-L-C-O-M-E   P-R-O-U-D

And then it happened. Drexel forgot for a moment how to spell Priscilla. There was a pause. The crowd waited and waited. Sir Blendalot began to fidget.

Then, Drexel's nose began to drip. It began to itch. His eyes filled up. And guess what happened? Drexel sneezed. The crowd went wild. Blendalot cheered. Proud Priscilla smiled.

Drexel had sneezed a huge ball of dragon fire. His

WELCOME PROUD PRISCILLA

was followed by a dragon fireworks display.

Drexel was a hero!

10

SKY WRITING—
DRAGON STYLE

(pages 7-10)

1. What is an allergy?

2. What did Sir Blendalot want Drexel to do?

3. How did Drexel feel about himself in the end?

4. Name the two words that make each compound word.

   saddlebag   cupcake   handkerchief
   watchmaker   sunset

5. Name the compound words you find in the story.

Why the Elephant's Trunk Is Long

Long ago, many elephants walked around the countryside. They looked like the elephants we know today, but they all had very short trunks.

One day Elwyn, the smallest elephant, said to his mother, "I wish to go to the water hole for a cool drink and a roll in the mud."

Lillie Elephant, his mother, said, "Be careful near the water hole. There are dangers hiding among the lovely plants."

"Dangers," laughed Elwyn. "Impossible! Nothing is dangerous to an elephant."

"Laugh all you want," said Mildred Monkey, a family friend, "but you just keep a sharp eye out for danger."

Elwyn lumbered off to the water hole to drink and play. Oh, what great fun it was to roll in the mud with his friends.

At last, it was time to go home. Elwyn walked to the water's edge to get one more drink. He stared at his face in the still water and said loudly, "How good-looking I am."

The noise woke up a crocodile sleeping in the bushes nearby. He yawned and looked around. And then he saw the juicy baby elephant.

Quick as a wink, the crocodile slipped into the water and grabbed Elwyn's short trunk in his strong crocodile jaws. The crocodile pulled and pulled toward the water. Elwyn pulled and pulled away from the water. The tug-of-war went on for three hours.

Elwyn's trunk began to stretch as the battle went on. The crocodile pulled and pulled. Elwyn pulled and pulled. And the trunk got longer and longer.

Finally, the crocodile grew tired of the battle. He let go of Elwyn's trunk. And what a trunk it was!

Elwyn fell to the ground. "My lovely trunk is ruined. How long it is!" cried Elwyn. The poor little elephant with the long trunk ran home, crying all the way.

"Oh, Mother! Oh, Father! Look what has happened to my beautiful short trunk."

"Easy, son. Don't get so upset. If we think hard, we can make it come out all right," said Barney Elephant. He looked at his son's big trunk, and he thought about the problem.

"I have it," said Barney. "Elwyn will start a whole new way of wearing a trunk. He'll wear his long trunk proudly, and soon everyone will want long trunks."

As the days passed, Elwyn found many ways to enjoy his new trunk. He could reach high into the trees for delicious things to eat. He could spray himself with cool water, and he could reach the ground without bending over.

Soon, all the elephants had heard of the new trunk. They came from miles around to marvel at Elwyn's good luck.

One by one, the elephants went to the water hole to have their trunks made long. Before they knew it, the crocodiles had time for nothing else but trunk pulling.

Before long, all the elephants were wearing long trunks like Elwyn's. And they were never happier. They were so thankful that they elected Elwyn the elephant president.

He ruled long with a long trunk. And he often said, "Sometimes it pays to stick your nose where it doesn't belong."

15

Why the Elephant's Trunk Is Long

(pages 12-15)

1. Is this story a good example of making the best of what you have? Why?

2. How did Elwyn use his new trunk?

3. What does "keep your nose out of it" mean?

4. Which word has a base word? Name the base word.
   danger   yawned   water

5. What are the base words?
   lumbered   walked   stared

ANSWERS

1. Yes. Elwyn was elected president because he made good use of his trunk.
2. He reached into trees and to the ground, and he sprayed himself with water.
3. Don't interfere when it's not your business.
4. yawn
5. lumber, walk, stare

A NOSE IS A BANANA

*You and your classmates have ways of saying things.
Here's the way some fourth-graders said things
they were thinking about.*

The Fruit Bowl

A nose is a banana except it is
          Yellow
A head is a pumpkin except it is
          Orange
A cheek is an apple except it has a
          Stem
A body is a fruit bowl because it has
          Everything

17

Mrs. Wiener and the Pretzel

To Mrs. Wiener
Crunching a pretzel
Waiting for the afternoon
When somebody will give her another
You can see how she likes it
Taking extremely large pieces
We should name this poem
Mrs. Wiener and the Pretzel.

Metaphors

The pretzel is a Mrs. Wiener.
The rose is a ripe cherry.
The wasp is a scream from my big sister.
A bee is a jump underneath the bed by my sister.
A cloud is a kitten playing with a breeze.
A breeze is a string for a cloud to play with.
Is the sun a ball of string which the breeze
   was cut from?
Maybe, but the breeze is blue and the sun is orange.
Do the cloud cats drink the rain?
Maybe, but do they like it?
No, because it isn't milk.

Mr. T.V.

Ho Mr. T.V. with a flick of my finger I see
   a movie or a colorful cartoon. I make you
   look funny.
Ho Mr. T.V. how does it feel to have an oil well
   in you?
Ho Mr. T.V. what is your favorite show?
Ho Mr. T.V. do you like mystery stories?
Or do you go looking at Chinese junks?
Do you owl at detective stories or at midnight
   do you show crisscross cars and go beepbeep?
Ho Mr. T.V. tell me in the big little voice
   of yours.

A NOSE IS A BANANA

(pages 17-20)

1. How did the poet know Mrs. Wiener liked the pretzel?

2. What fruits are named in the first poem?

3. In the third poem, why didn't the cloud cats like the rain?

4. Pick the word that has an inflected ending.
       jelly   extremely   pretzel   label

5. Pick the words that have inflected endings.
       detects   finger   color   waiting

1. She took extremely large pieces.
2. banana, pumpkin, apple
3. because it isn't milk
4. extremely
5. detects, waiting

ANSWERS

HAIKU: A ONE-BREATH POEM

Haiku is the Japanese word for "short poem."
Haiku . . . a "one-breath poem" . . . tells
about one special feeling, or one tiny time,
or one precious thought.

In *A Few Flies and I,* Issa, the poet, pinpoints
his feelings in very few words.

When he was six, he wrote:

Come,
Motherless sparrows,
And play
With me.

And when he was older:

O owl!
Change your expression,
In the spring rain!

He even wrote about those little pests:

The mosquitoes!
They have come for their lunch
To the man having a nap.

A few flies
And I
Keep house together
In this humble home.

Listen as the poet talks:

People are few;
A leaf falls here,
Falls there.

Just being here,
I am here,
And the snow falls.

HAIKU: A ONE-BREATH POEM

(pages 22-25)

1. What will be the mosquitoes' lunch?

2. What does <u>haiku</u> mean?

3. Why is the phrase "a one-breath poem" a good way to describe haiku?

4. Find the ending for the word.
   In the last poem, the poet was reflect_____.
        ly   ful   ing

5. Find the ending for the word.
   The poet tells us, "A leaf fall___ here."
        ed   s   ing   es

5. s
4. ing
3. Haiku tells about one short thought or feeling which you can read in one breath.
2. short poem
1. the man who is having a nap

26

ANSWERS

EVIL, PRINCE OF PREFIXES, and HAPPY KING HENRY

PART I

Happy King Henry and smiling Queen Irene ruled the happy kingdom of Happyland. Every day they stood at the window of their palace and made a happy speech to all the happy people in Happyland.

"Good morning, all my happy friends," yelled happy King Henry. "I love you all. Do you love me?"

And all together, like one big, happy team, the people of Happyland yelled back, "Yes!" And all together, they smiled. So many smiles at one time made the whole of Happyland sparkle and shine.

Two people did not smile. At the back of the palace were Evil, Prince of Prefixes, in his dark knickers, and Norman No No, Prince Evil's nasty friend. Prince Evil never laughed. He just snickered.

Structural Analysis **6**

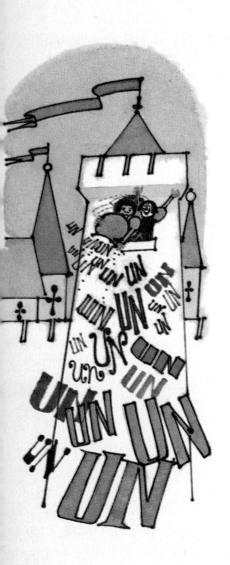

"Oh boy! Oh boy!" said Norman No No. "When you snicker in your knickers, I know you are going to do something mean. What will it be?"

Twisting his mean mustache, Prince Evil snickered, "Snicker, snicker, I will take all this happiness away from Happyland. Quickly, naughty Norman, get my Mean Prefix Bag."

Norman No No thrust his hand deep into the prefix bag. "I feel lots of no-no's in there. Look! I have a fistful of <u>un</u>s and a great big <u>dis</u>. <u>Un</u> means <u>not</u>, and <u>dis</u> means <u>not</u>."

Prince Evil snickered and twisted his mustache. "Take the <u>un</u>s, Norman. Pour them out of the palace tower, and we will fill the land with <u>un</u>happiness. Happyland will be <u>Un</u>happyland. But before you go," snarled Prince Evil, "leave a handful of <u>un</u>s with me. I have another evil thing to do."

Norman No No waited for a big wind and then let fly with all his biggest, juiciest, meanest <u>un</u>s.

That night the mean Prince Evil waited at the King's bedroom window until the happy King walked by. Then he threw a fistful of <u>uns</u> on the King's head.

Pow! The poor King never knew what hit him. Suddenly he was covered with <u>uns</u> from head to toe.

"Heh, heh!" snickered Prince Evil. "The King has had it. He is <u>un-ed</u>."

(When someone is <u>un-ed</u>, it doesn't show at all. The magic spelling of <u>un</u> is so strong that no one knows who is <u>un-ed</u> and who is not.)

The King did not know he had been <u>un-ed</u>. He turned to Queen Irene and said, "Just looking at you makes me <u>un</u>happy."

The Queen could not believe her ears.

The King continued, "I am so <u>un</u>lucky to have you as my Queen."

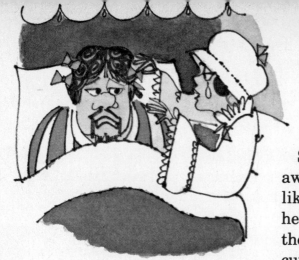

Smiling Queen Irene felt awful. The King never acted like this. A tear rolled down her cheek as she helped put the King's hair up in curlers.

The King turned in the bed and said, "My dear, after you have <u>un</u>curled my hair, please <u>un</u>cover me, give me my <u>un</u>friendly teddy bear, and be sure to <u>un</u>lock the door for the night!"

"Oh dear, oh dear," Queen Irene sobbed.

"How very <u>un</u>pleasant of you," said the King, as he fell asleep.

And that night, <u>un</u>smiling Queen Irene cried. She cried until she fell asleep and dreamed. In her dream, the <u>un</u>selfish Good Fairy came to her and said,

"My dear Queen Irene,
The King is not mean.
The Evil Prefix Prince
Will make you wince.
He'll make fair <u>un</u>fair,
So of him just beware."

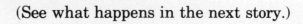

(See what happens in the next story.)

EVIL, PRINCE OF PREFIXES, and HAPPY KING HENRY

Part 1 (pages 27-30)

1. What is a snicker?

2. What happened when all the people smiled together?

3. Who was in Queen Irene's dream?

4. Pick the word that has the prefix.
   uncle   uncover   under   umpire

5. All of the following words have a prefix except

   _____ .

   unlucky   unpleasant   morning   disagree

5. morning
4. uncover
3. the Good Fairy
2. The whole of Happyland sparkled and shone.
1. a half-suppressed laugh, often disrespectful

31   ANSWERS

EVIL, PRINCE OF PREFIXES, and HAPPY KING HENRY

PART II

In the last story, Evil, Prince of Prefixes, threw some <u>un</u>s from his Prefix Bag at happy King Henry. Since <u>un</u> means <u>not</u>, King Henry suddenly became <u>un</u>pleasant to Queen Irene. She had a dream which told her to beware of the Prince.

The next morning, the crowd gathered as usual under the palace window. Hiding in the shadows were Prince Evil and Norman No No.

"Quickly, Norman," said the Prince, "give me the great big <u>dis</u> from our Prefix Bag. The King is about to speak."

Norman gave Prince Evil the <u>dis</u> prefix, which means <u>not</u>.

"Here it goes," said the Prince as he hurled the negative prefix <u>dis</u> toward the King. It splashed over the King as he began to speak.

"Good morning, my <u>dis</u>loyal subjects. It is my <u>dis</u>pleasure to see all of you here this morning," said the King.

The crowd was shocked. Could this be their beloved King speaking?

The King continued, "I know you <u>dis</u>agree with all I have to say. I know this because I am sure of your <u>dis</u>trust. Both the Queen and I <u>dis</u>like all of you because we know that each of you is <u>dis</u>honest and <u>dis</u>obeys all the laws of our kingdom."

The unhappy crowd cried out in <u>dis</u>approval. What could be the matter with their beloved King?

The <u>dis</u>believing, unsmiling Queen dragged the puzzled King away from the window. She knew that the King was under the evil spelling spell of Prince Evil.

"My wonderful King," said the Queen, "you have a strange illness. You have a breakdown in your prefixing. Only the Great Syllabicator can cure you."

So a call went out for the Great Syllabicator, and she was brought to the palace.

The Queen explained the problem. The Great One listened carefully.

"Ah, so!" said the Great Syllabicator. "Someone has tampered with the King's prefixes, but how are his suffixes?"

"Suffixes?" asked the Queen."What are suffixes?"

The Great Syllabicator said, "Surely you know that a suffix is a syllable attached to the rear of a word. It changes the meaning of that word. We'll use suffixes to cure the King."

And with three pills, two magic drinks and sixteen thumps on the King's head, the Great Syllabicator took the <u>uns</u> and the great big <u>dis</u> and threw in some suffixes.

<u>Dis</u>pleasure became pleasur<u>able</u>, and <u>un</u>loved changed to lov<u>able</u>. <u>Dis</u>agree became agree<u>able</u>; <u>dis</u>trust became trust<u>ing</u>. <u>Un</u>friendly became friendl<u>iness</u>, <u>dis</u>like became lik<u>able</u> and, of course, <u>un</u>happy became happ<u>iness</u>.

Queen Irene smiled her biggest, sparkling smile. The people of Happyland cheered and laughed and loved.

"Now," said the Great Syllabicator, "I shall <u>un</u>cover Evil, Prince of Prefixes, and his nasty Norman No No."

It didn't take her long to find them. "Aha! There's

where you word-wiggling, prefix-puffing, language looters are hiding."

Poor Prince of Prefixes and Norman No No were not <u>un</u>afraid, which means they were very scared.

"I will fix you forever," said the Great Syllabicator. "I'll fix you, Norman No No, with a little bit of magic spelling. Hear this magic chant.

"Letters large and letters small,
Do a job to help us all.
Change this Norman No No mess
From Norman No No to Norman Yes."

And from that day on, <u>un</u>friendly, <u>un</u>loved, nasty Norman No No became friend<u>ly</u>, lov<u>able</u> Norman Yes. He always said yes.

The Great Syllabicator turned to Evil, Prince of Prefixes. "You! I'll fix you forever. I'll fix you with a suffix that will change your ways." And she said the magic spelling chant:

"Letters large and letters small,
Let us end this once and for all.
Prince Evil's name is an evil mess,
So change it now to Prince Evil-<u>less</u>."

And with one suffix, the Great Syllabicator made Evil, Prince of Prefixes, into Evil-<u>less</u>, Prince of Suffixes. Everyone smiled.

EVIL, PRINCE OF PREFIXES, and HAPPY KING HENRY

Part II (pages 32-35)

1. What does the word <u>syllabicate</u> mean?

2. What was used to cure the King?

3. What was Prince Evil's new name?

4. Pick the word that has the suffix.
    stable   syllable   agreeable

5. Pick the two words with suffixes.
    trusting   stress
    king   table
    happiness

PROUD ZACHARY
THE MAGNIFICENT ZEBRA

PART I

"A bit dry, my friend. These grass goodies are a bit dry." Zachary Zebra munched on the hay that Mr. Corpulent, the zookeeper, gave him.

Zachary's old pal, Arenta Zebra, kept chewing and looked at her friend's magnificent stripes. Proud Zachary was by far the most magnificent zebra in the zoo. Everyone knew it. Zachary knew it, too.

"Tell me, Arenta, what do you want for Christmas? Have you made up your list yet?" Zachary kept munching and talking with his mouth full. Arenta said nothing.

"I have a long list of things I want." Zachary kept munching and talking. "My list," he said proudly, "is a mile long. How long is yours? Come on, Arenta, say something."

"Not with my mouth full," said Arenta, after she ate a mouthful. "And, if I stop eating to talk, you will finish all the goodies. So you talk, and I'll just eat."

"Well, first I want a big can of stripe polish. That will keep my stripes shining and beautiful; then everyone will love me even more than they do now. I want a hard brush to keep my zebra hair neat and a soft brush to keep my neat hair shining. I will need a mirror to see my magnificent self," said Zachary, hay dripping from the sides of a mouth that never seemed to shut.

"Come on, Arenta, you must want a lot of things for Christmas, too."

"No," said Arenta Zebra, as she bent down for more hay. "No," she said one more time, just before she took another mouthful.

"Arenta, all you do is eat. Why don't you talk more? The hay is all gone now. Let me — "

Arenta did not wait for Zachary to say more. Arenta just looked up and said, "Who has time to talk when you are around? You do all the talking."

"I want some new zebra shoes, and a pair of zebra sunglasses and a big zebra hat that my beautiful ears can stick out of," Zachary went on. "Now tell me, Arenta, what is on your list? Tell me. Tell me."

"Nothing," said Arenta, "nothing at all."

Zachary did not seem to hear his pal. "And, after all those nice things, I want a picture of me painted by Michael Antelope, the zoo artist. We can hang it over the zoo gate for all to see."

Then Zachary stopped talking. He looked at Arenta. "Arenta," said Zachary, "did you say 'nothing'? There is *nothing* you want for Christmas?"

"Nothing," said Arenta. "There are zebras and lions and elephants and all kinds of animals all over who need hay and grass. So this year I will give *them* things for Christmas. That will make me happy. I think, Zachary, that you are a bore. All you think about is yourself. You are very beautiful, Zachary, but you *are* a bore."

"A bore, am I!" Zachary was angry. "I am a beautiful zebra. Everyone comes to see me. Arenta, if that is how you feel, we cannot be pals. You will be sorry. I will show you how everyone loves me."

And so Zachary Zebra, looking in the zoo mirror, left his pal. "I'll show you. I'll show you how everyone loves me," said Zachary.

Psst! Poor Zachary. I'm still his pal. He'll need me soon. Read the next story and see what happens.

PROUD ZACHARY
THE MAGNIFICENT ZEBRA

Part I (pages 37-40)

1. Which words describe Zachary?
   conceited   generous   vain   magnanimous

2. Why didn't Arenta want to talk?

3. What do you think Zachary will do when he leaves Arenta?

4. How many syllables are in each word?
   a. Zachary   c. Christmas
   b. beautiful   d. polish

5. How many syllables are in each word?
   a. magnificent   c. talked
   b. proud   d. proudly

PROUD ZACHARY
THE MAGNIFICENT ZEBRA

PART II

In the last story, Arenta Zebra told Zachary Zebra he was a bore. Zachary left in a huff.

Zachary Zebra laughed in the funny way that zebras laugh. "Am I not the most magnificent animal in the zoo?" he asked, looking at his face in the mirror.

"You are not," came a voice from behind a bush by the side of the lake. "You are not so hot. Your face is too long. Your back is full of stripes. And what's more, you are a bore. You are a four-legged zebra bore. You are the biggest bore in the zoo. And you are not a bit as magnificent as I am."

Zachary was very angry. He was up on his hind legs and ready to fight. "Who are you? What are you? Who do you think you are? I am Zachary, the magnificent zebra, and no one is more beautiful than I."

"You are a bore. Nothing more than a bore," said the voice from behind the bush.

"Come out! Come out and fight! You cannot be more beautiful than I. Everyone loves me. Love me or fight."

"I think I will fight. I am more beautiful than you. Look out, you big bore. Here I come," said the voice behind the bush.

And out of the bush came Peter Peacock. Tiny Peter was not very pretty and not very big. In fact, he was so small that big Zachary could not even see him.

"Where? Where are you? I don't see you," said the zebra.

"Down here, you big bore. Look down. Here I am."

"You! Little ugly you? You think you are more beautiful than I? That is funny. That is so funny. Your nose has a point. Your head has a point. Your eyes are too small. You stick out all over. I can't fight you. You are too small and too ugly. I am too magnificent to bother with you."

And Zachary Zebra began to laugh. He laughed and laughed. He laughed so hard, he fell on the grass. How funny it was to Zachary!

"To think," said the big zebra, "to think that such a little bird has any idea that he could be as magnificent as a big zebra like me. You are a silly little bird. What kind of bird *are* you?"

"A peacock, you big fool," said Peter. And with that, he opened out all his feathers in a fan behind him. "I am Peter, the Magnificent Peacock, and you are a big bore.

"You are not so magnificent," the peacock went on. "Just look at me. Look at my feathers. Look how beautiful I can be. I may not be big. But, when I open out all my feathers, your shiny stripes are not as magnificent as all my beautiful feathers. You don't have to be big to be beautiful," said Peter Peacock.

Psst! I think I'll look on the other side of the zoo. Over there, I'll be magnificent. See me in the next story.

PROUD ZACHARY
THE MAGNIFICENT ZEBRA

Part II (pages 42-45)

1. Where was Peter hiding?

2. Why wouldn't Zachary fight Peter Peacock?

3. Did Peter let out his feathers before or after Zachary called him "ugly"?

4. Look out for this word. How many syllables in <u>legged</u>?

5. How many syllables are in each word?
   a. biggest   c. tiny
   b. peacock   d. ugly

ANSWERS

1. behind a bush by the side of the lake
2. Zachary was too magnificent to bother with him.
   He thought Peter was too small and too ugly.
3. after
4. 2
5. a. 2   b. 2   c. 2   d. 2

PROUD ZACHARY THE MAGNIFICENT ZEBRA

PART III

In the last story, Peter Peacock showed Zachary Zebra that beautiful does not mean big.

"That old peacock can have the lake," Zachary Zebra said to himself. "I'll take the rest of the zoo. I am the most magnificent animal in all the zoo, and everybody knows it, except that Peter Peacock."

Zachary turned to face the lake. He yelled, "You're not fair, Peacock. I did not want to talk about *your* good looks. I came over there to talk about *my* good looks. It just wasn't very nice. Have you no manners?"

There was no sound, except for the wind. And the wind seemed to say, "Bore. Bore."

"Everyone knows. Everyone knows," Zachary kept saying to himself. And he sat down by the big tree where the zoo birds lived.

Structural Analysis **10**

"Everyone knows what?" asked Bertha Blue Jay from the branch above the zebra's head.

"Everyone knows that I—I—" And before Zachary could finish, Bertha began chattering.

"I? Eyes? Oh, yes, my eyes. I *do* have beautiful dark eyes. Don't you just love my eyes?" And without waiting for Zachary to answer, she kept up her chatter.

"Everyone knows I am the most beautiful bird in the zoo. Do you see how beautiful my new tail feathers are? We're wearing them longer this year. What do you think? Are mine the right shade of blue for my eyes?"

Poor Zachary Zebra could only say, "I—I—"

Without stopping, the blue jay went on, "Would my feathers look better with purple? Are they straight? Do they have the proper shine?

"You must see my new nest," the bird went on. "It's up there to the left. It's the latest in split-level nests, you know. There's not another one like it in the zoo."

Zachary tried to change the subject. "Would you like to see my Christmas list?" he asked quickly.

But Bertha did not hear him. "You must see the pictures of my latest eggs. Aren't they cute?" said Bertha, holding up two pictures. "The doctor says they are big and beautiful for their age.

"Hugo, the younger, will be good at worm-finding like his father. Hilda, his sister, will be very good at stick-finding. I'm good at finding twigs, too. Both will be very bright when they grow up. I would—"

"Stop! Stop!" Zachary cried, unable to stand it any longer. "All you think about is yourself. You are beautiful, Bertha, but you are a bore! All you talk about is yourself. You must stop this and think of others. I cannot stand you!"

"Oh, that's too bad," sighed Bertha, "because I've got my family photo album right here under my wing. There are the most darling pictures of my grandparents when they were young. Are you sure you can't stand just a little more?"

But Zachary was not there to answer. He was on his way back to where the zebras lived.

"Arenta! Arenta! My old pal, where are you?" Zachary called. "Where are you, my beautiful pal? I need you."

Zachary Zebra could not find his friend. He did not see Arenta, Peter Peacock and Bertha Blue Jay behind the big oak tree that sits in the middle of the zoo. But you can see them here. Can you guess what they did?

PROUD ZACHARY
THE MAGNIFICENT ZEBRA

Part III (pages 47-50)

1. Who was Zachary's match? What does "meet his match" mean?

2. What did Zachary's friends do in the last picture?

3. What did the wind seem to say to Zachary?

4. Divide <u>magnificent</u> into syllables.

5. Divide these words into syllables.
   zebra   Bertha   branch

ANSWERS

1. Bertha Blue Jay; Zachary meets someone who equals him.
2. They had planned to show Zachary how boring he was and were laughing about it.
3. "Bore, Bore."
4. mag-nif-i-cent
5. ze-bra   Ber-tha   branch

A BALLOON
FOR EVERY
BABOON

This is a baboon.
She is one big monkey.

This is a buffoon.
He is one silly fool.

This is a balloon.
This is one bag of hot air.

Bobbie Baboon,
a buffoon with a balloon.

Bobbie Baboon was a buffoon. She was one silly fool. She was a foolish baboon. So then everyone called Bobbie Baboon a buffoon.

"You're a babbling buffoon," said Barbara Baboon.

"You're a babbling bore. You're a buffoon baboon," said Barbara and Boris and even Belinda Baboon. While all the baboons looked mean, Bobbie played with her balloon.

"I'm not. I'm really not such a fool," Bobbie answered. "I just don't like to do what all baboons do. I'm a balloon baboon, not a big bad baboon. I'd rather play with my balloon than be that kind of baboon."

While all the baboons looked for nuts and fruit to eat, Bobbie Baboon floated around the big rock where the baboons lived.

While all the baboons chased the other animals away, Bobbie just floated and floated.

"She's full of hot air," said Brenda Baboon.

"Just like her balloon," said Betty Baboon, as she patted Baby Beebee Baboon on her back. "My Baby Beebee will grow up to swing through the trees. She won't need hot air to keep herself up."

One day, Big Boris Baboon, the baboon boss, went up to the top of the rock. He called all the baboons together. The whole baboon troop—baboons come in troops, not bunches—gathered around their boss.

"People," said Boris, "lots of strong, strange, stomping people are coming. They don't even have tails. They are coming to build their houses. We must get out now, before they make monkeys out of us."

"They'll put us in a zoo," said Betty.

"They'll make us into monkey bread," said Bernard Baboon. Bernard was a baboon baker.

So the troop had to move. The females and baby baboons went to the middle of a big circle. The male baboons stayed around the outside of the circle. They kept the baby baboons safe and sound. All together in a big circle, the two hundred baboons in the troop moved down to the river. A big rock and tall trees were on the other side of the river.

"That's our new home," said Boris, the Big Boss.

"It's beautiful," said Betty. "But how do we get across? Baboons can't swim."

Bobbie Baboon, that big buffoon who floated with her balloon, saved the troop. Do you know what she did?

A BALLOON
FOR EVERY BABOON

(pages 52-55)

1. How do you think the baboons felt about Bobbie at the end of the story?

2. What does it mean when someone says you are "full of hot air"?

3. What made Boris decide that the baboon troop had to move?

4. What word does Barbara Baboon use that means <u>you are</u>?

5. Match the contractions with their words.

   I'd   do not
   don't   I am
   I'm   I would

5. I'd—I would, don't—do not, I'm—I am
4. you're
3. People were coming.
2. You talk too much.
1. They did not think she was a fool.
   They were thankful she had a balloon.

ANSWERS

56

TERRY TUNA'S TRICK

This is Maxine Mackerel.
A mackerel is a small fish.

This is Terry Tuna.
A tuna is a big fish.

"No! No, Maxine. Don't touch that worm," Terry Tuna cried out. "It's on a hook. If you bite, you'll end up on a dish!"

Maxine Mackerel turned away from the hook. "I'm hungry, Terry. My tummy is empty. I need a good worm breakfast before I go to work."

"If you go after that worm, you'll never get to work," Terry Tuna warned. "There's a hook, line, rod and person at the other end. If you bite the worm, that person will put you on a dish. Stay away from the worm, or you'll end up in that person's tummy."

Maxine moved away. She looked at her fish watch. "Well, I guess I have some time to hunt for something to eat down at the bottom of the sea. But I wish those people up there wouldn't hand out their juicy worms. It's so easy to grab a bite."

57

"I think we should do something about those hooks," Terry Tuna thought. "It isn't right for people to hang their hooks down here for us to bite. I think we should teach those people a lesson or two."

"Why not?" asked Maxine Mackerel. "I work at a school. I have a lot of students. A whole school of mackerel should be able to think of something to do!"

"I have it! I know what we can do," Terry said, jumping up from her sea shell. "We'll teach people one good lesson. We'll all go peopling."

Maxine looked at her friend. "We'll go what? We'll go where? We'll go how?"

"Peopling! Peopling! People go fishing, so fish will go peopling." Terry really meant what she said. "Maxine, you get all your students. Go get your school of mackerel. Bring all your students back here. We'll show those people."

"This way, my mackerel students," Maxine said. "Terry is waiting for us. We're going peopling. Terry says we'll teach people something they won't forget."

"Now," said Terry, "we are going to make a tall tower—a mackerel tower." She had each mackerel stand on top of another mackerel.

When the people saw the mackerel tail sticking out of the water, they got all excited. "Fish! Fish!" they yelled.

One man got so excited that he dropped his fishing pole and jumped into the water. "I'll get that fish," he yelled. "It's mine, and I'll get it."

Guess who got whom?

As soon as the man hit the water, the whole school of mackerel got him.

They pulled him to a big people dish at the bottom of the sea. "We'll show them," said Terry.

Oliver Octopus held the poor man on the dish. All the other fish watched and waited.

59

"Let's eat! Let's eat!" cried all the fish. "This looks better than a fat worm. Man, oh man, this looks like good meat to eat."

The man cried out, "Don't eat me! Please, don't eat me!"

The fish did not think they'd like man meat anyway. So, they didn't eat him. No, they didn't.

Oliver Octopus let go, and that poor man swam as fast as any man could swim.

And do you know what the fish did as soon as the man reached the boat? Just look and see.

TERRY TUNA'S TRICK

(pages 57-60)

1. What does "peopling" mean?

2. What did the fish want to show the people?

3. How did Terry make a mackerel tower?

4. Pick the phrase that has a contraction.
   - Terry's trick
   - Let's eat.
   - person's tummy

5. Find all the contractions on the first page of this story.

ANSWERS

Sooner or Later,
Sounds Make a Difference

Wendy Whale doesn't like people. Why should she? For years, Wendy has heard stories of people hunting whales to get whale oil, whalebone and whale skin.

Peggy Porpoise likes people. Playful Peggy thinks a lot like people. She catches fish from people. She likes to swim alongside boats and beg for food. Some people think Peggy is even smarter than people.

Terry Tuna plays tricks. She is always up to some kind of mischief.

One day Terry Tuna was singing a tune, a tuna tune. Tunas do that now and then.

Whales and porpoises love sounds. So Wendy Whale and Peggy Porpoise came swimming around.

"Great tune, Terry," said Wendy.

"Fine tuna tune," said Peggy. "Let's hear it again. One more time, Terry, for the fish on the other coast." Sounds can travel far underwater.

Here is Terry's song.

Take a tip from Terry Tuna,
Sing a tuna tune–er.
Sing it now or sing it then,
But try to sing it *sooner*.

"Oh, wow!" laughed Wendy. "That tuna tune is a hit. Fish will sing it all over the sea. We'll hear it on fish radio and on fish TV. We'll hear it from shore to shore."

"Something's fishy," said Peggy. "Something very fishy is going on here. Why do you sing the word *sooner* so loudly?"

"I sing the highest notes on *sooner,* and it's the only way I can hit those notes," Terry explained with a sly smile. And she sang her tune over and over again.

Wendy Whale sang Terry's tune. And they both sang the high notes on *sooner* very loudly.

"Oh, that swings," said Wendy. "I love it. I love that swinging tune. Tune–er sooner! That's too much!" And Wendy danced that silly dance that whales sometimes dance.

Now, as Wendy Whale sang, Terry Tuna laughed. And Peggy Porpoise said, "It's all too fishy."

That's when it happened. Suddenly a big sailing ship, called a schooner, came along.

Poor Wendy Whale. She was so busy singing Terry Tuna's new hit tune that she did not see the schooner until it was almost on top of her. You know how frightened Wendy is of people. She almost jumped out of her whale skin.

Peggy Porpoise said, "Don't be afraid, Wendy. People are nice. Come with me and see."

They *were* nice. The people threw food to the whale and the porpoise. But Peggy still thought something was fishy.

"How did you know we were here?" Peggy asked the sailor on the schooner.

"Someone here kept yelling, schooner, schooner, schooner," said the sailor. "We thought someone was calling us."

"That was *sooner*, not *schooner*," said Wendy. "Right, Terry?"

"Right," said Terry with a wink. "But now you got to see that people are nice after all."

Sooner or Later,
Sounds Make a Difference

(pages 62-65)

1. Why didn't Wendy Whale like people?

2. What else did Terry Tuna like to do besides play tricks?

3. What trick did Terry play on Wendy Whale?

4. Match the picture with the right word.

    porpoise
    purpose
    porpoises

5. Find all the plural words on the second page of the story.

HOW THE SEA GOT ITS SALT

(based on a Norse legend)

There once were two sisters, one rich and one poor. On Christmas Eve the poor one came to the rich one and begged for some food. "Only if you do what I say," said the mean rich sister. "If you do what I say, I'll give you some bacon."

The poor sister agreed, and the rich sister gave her some bacon and snarled, "Take it and go to the Devil."

And the poor honest sister was not one to break a promise. She went out looking for the Devil. On her way, she met an old man with a long white beard who asked her where she was going.

"Oh, I'm going to the Devil, if I can find the right way to get there."

"You're almost there already," said the old man. "Just knock at that door. But if you go in with that bacon, all the devils will want it, for there is very little meat in that place. Sell it to them, but take the little hand grinder behind the door for your payment. Then come to me and I will show you how to use it, for it is not easy."

Well, the Devil did not want to part with the grinder, but he wanted the bacon very badly. So he finally gave in after a lot of haggling. And the old man showed the poor sister how to use the magic grinder.

She got home just in time for her small Christmas Eve dinner—two boiled potatoes. "This grinder will provide much more than that," she said to herself. And sure enough, following the old man's instructions, the grinder poured out a great feast. And after the feast, it poured out a storehouse full of food, new clothes, three new wagons, four cows that gave milk, sixty-three chickens, forty-seven hens and a canary.

When the rich sister saw what the grinder could do, she paid her sister a thousand coins for the magic grinder.

But she did not wait to learn how to use it. When she got home she ordered the grinder to grind out some cereal and milk for supper. The grinder started producing milk and cereal. It produced and produced. The sister didn't know how to stop it. Soon the whole kitchen was under cereal and milk. Then the living room, all the bedrooms and the barn, too. Cereal and milk poured out of the windows into the sister's fields. Soon she had an ocean of cereal and milk.

She ran to her sister and begged, "Take back the magic grinder." The poor sister (remember, she was now richer than the rich sister) did—for another two thousand coins. And, of course, she got the grinder to stop.

Well, the good sister used that grinder for many years. And she got very rich. She got famous, too—at least her grinder got famous.

One day a greedy sea captain, who was in the salt business, came to her and asked if the magic grinder could grind out salt.

"Of course it can," said the good sister. "It can grind out anything." And she made it grind out salt.

The greedy captain saw how to make it grind out salt, so he stole the magic grinder and sailed away on his ship. He began grinding out salt. That little old grinder started pouring out tons and tons of salt. The greedy captain knew how to start it working, but he never learned how to stop it. So when the salt covered his whole ship, and the ship started to sink, the upset captain grabbed the magic grinder, screamed in anger, "Go to the Devil!" and threw the grinder overboard just before his ship sank.

Now that grinder and the ship sit somewhere at the bottom of the sea. The ship rusts and rots, but the grinder just keeps grinding out salt.

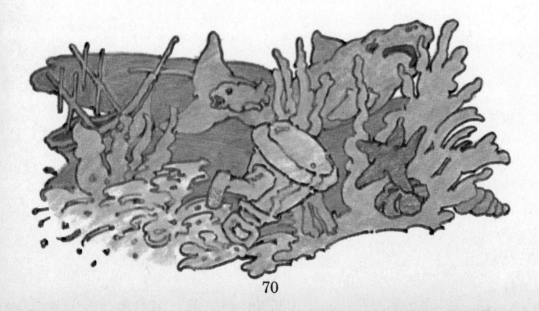

HOW THE SEA GOT ITS SALT

(pages 67-70)

1. What did the greedy captain do just before his ship sank?

2. Why did the Devil finally part with the grinder?

3. Which sister had the magic grinder first?

4. What are the singular forms of these words?
   sisters   shoes   fields

5. Pick the word that does not have a singular form.
   potatoes   wagons   clothes

ANSWERS

THE FLYING MACHINE

Imagine that it is 1776, and we are traveling from New York City to Philadelphia, a distance of ninety-three miles.

We rock back and forth in a constant motion. Our backs ache from sitting so long in one spot.

Four spirited horses pull our canvas-covered express coach through mud and rocks along deer and Indian trails. Fallen trees and overflowing rivers block the roads. When the rivers are not too high, we ford them. Otherwise, we ride until we find one of the few bridges.

The summer sun beats down on the crowded coach. Naturally, there is no air conditioning. By midday we are hungry, too.

The restaurant at a wayside inn is nothing like the modern diners that dot today's superhighways. This restaurant smells of poorly prepared food. Crammed together on a bench, we stuff sauerkraut, knockwurst, creamed potato salad and beer into cast-iron stomachs. Then quickly, we go back to the hot, crowded coach and the bumpy roads.

At night the coach driver makes another stop. No clean, bright, new motels with baths await us. Nor is there any town to shelter or entertain us. Instead, we all bunk in a log cabin—a private house that takes in travelers. There is no tile bathroom for washing up and no indoor plumbing, so we use the outhouse. If we're lucky, we can share a bed with strangers, or, if there are no beds left, we put blankets on the hearth and use saddles for pillows.

Outside the cabin, a bear bangs and scratches at the door, trying to get in. A wolf howls in the distance as we fall asleep.

The next morning, a large dog watches us hungrily as we eat our breakfast of bacon and eggs. Noisy young children run about.

After breakfast, it's back to the hot, crowded coach. The driver uses his ax to clear away fallen trees. Sometimes it is too wet to travel, so we pull off to the side of the road and wait for the mud to dry.

Soon we are close to town and the roads are a little better. We stop at an inn for lunch. The people at the inn ask us questions. They are eager for news from a faraway place.

It takes a long time for news to travel in 1776, without telephones or TV. A letter takes from three to ten weeks to arrive. There are no stamps. The person who gets the letter must pay for the delivery.

Finally, after a day and a half of traveling, the coach arrives.

"Everyone off," the driver shouts. We haven't slept well, and we are very tired. Our clothing is creased and dirty. Our stomachs grumble. We are hungry again. Our legs are like rubber as we get off the coach in Philadelphia.

We have just taken a long, difficult and dangerous trip in another time, about two hundred years ago. We are in the American colonies in 1776. We have traveled ninety-three miles at the average speed of three miles an hour on a new coach line called The Flying Machine. It has two departures a week in the winter and three in the summer.

Perhaps some of our traveling companions were delegates to the Continental Congress. They might have been going to Philadelphia to vote on and sign the Declaration of Independence. Maybe we were on a famous trip in The Flying Machine. We'll never know.

What did the American colonies become? How much do you know about the Declaration of Independence? Have you ever gone ninety-three miles away from home? Where did you go? How long did it take you? How did you go? With whom? How fast did you go? Why do you think it takes so much less time now to travel places? What has changed? What improvements are there?

People have always enjoyed going places. Think how much easier it is nowadays.

THE FLYING MACHINE

(pages 72-75)

1. Why was there no air conditioning?

2. Why did the people at the inn ask the travelers questions?

3. How many miles an hour did The Flying Machine travel?

4. Pick the plural words.
   miles   beds
   it's   sleeps

5. Find the plural words on the last page of the story.

ANSWERS

1. It hadn't been invented yet.
2. They were eager for news from a faraway place.
3. three
4. miles, beds
5. years, miles, departures, companions, colonies, delegates, places, improvements, people

UP FOR GRABS–
A
GIRAFFE STORY

The sun was low in the winter sky. Marty Smarty hoped her sneakers would carry her safely home.

She was late because Mr. Stern had asked her to mark spelling tests after school. That was because Marty Smarty always got a hundred on her spelling tests.

Slap, slap, slap, went Marty's sneakers on the wet sidewalk. She slowed down as she saw the shadows on a pile of trash cans. Was that tall, skinny shadow moving?

Marty was scared. "Who are you?" she called fearfully.

"P_ p_ p_ please, miss," said a tiny voice that seemed to travel a long way from up above, "please, miss, have you a home for a homeless baby giraffe?"

Marty was stunned. "You're kidding!" she said. "Not a real giraffe!"

Structural Analysis 16

"Yes," said the tiny voice. "Jason's my name, Jason Giraffe. I eat plants and leaves, and I won't need a bed—I can sleep standing up. I hardly make any noise. I love children . . ."

"You're beautiful," Marty interrupted. "Your spots are just beautiful."

"Then you'll take me home with you?" Jason asked hopefully, as he fell into step with Marty. They walked side by side while Marty thought about Jason's request.

She didn't have to think long. A beautiful giraffe was something very special.

Marty made a deal with Jason. "You can stay in my room if you're quiet," she said, "and I'll keep you there as long as no one knows."

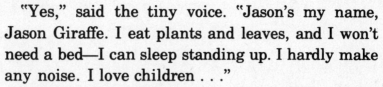

The first night wasn't too hard. Marty sneaked Jason into her room while Mom bathed Marty's baby sister. Jason had to lower his head to get under the doorway.

Jason stuck his head out the window and ate some leaves from a tree.

And when Dad came to tuck Marty into bed, Jason put a lampshade on his head.

When Marty's father left, Jason closed his eyes. He was almost asleep when Marty's mother was at the door.

"Quick, Jason," Marty said. "Get under the lampshade again, and don't move."

"I just came to say goodnight," said Mom. "But your lamp! Why did you paint those spots all over it? It looks funny."

"I like it," Marty said, and her mother left.

The real trouble began the next day. Poor Jason was bored standing around with a lampshade on his head, waiting for Marty to get home from school. And he was hungry, too. He had eaten all the leaves from the tree outside Marty's window.

He looked out the window and saw a woman wearing a big, flowered hat. There were lots of green leaves on it, too. He stuck his head out the window and grabbed the hat from the woman's head. The woman stomped to Marty's door.

Marty's mother opened the door, and the woman said, "A giraffe took my hat. Please look for it."

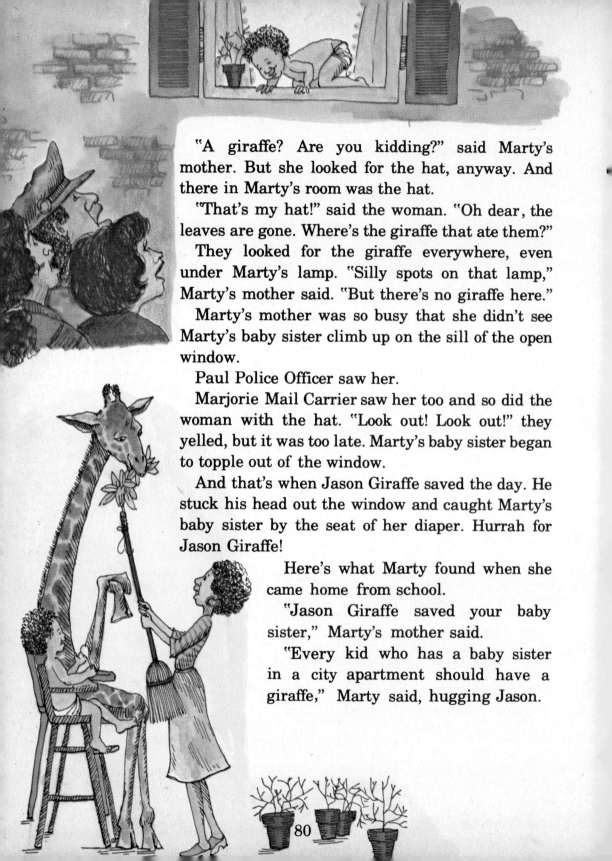

"A giraffe? Are you kidding?" said Marty's mother. But she looked for the hat, anyway. And there in Marty's room was the hat.

"That's my hat!" said the woman. "Oh dear, the leaves are gone. Where's the giraffe that ate them?"

They looked for the giraffe everywhere, even under Marty's lamp. "Silly spots on that lamp," Marty's mother said. "But there's no giraffe here."

Marty's mother was so busy that she didn't see Marty's baby sister climb up on the sill of the open window.

Paul Police Officer saw her.

Marjorie Mail Carrier saw her too and so did the woman with the hat. "Look out! Look out!" they yelled, but it was too late. Marty's baby sister began to topple out of the window.

And that's when Jason Giraffe saved the day. He stuck his head out the window and caught Marty's baby sister by the seat of her diaper. Hurrah for Jason Giraffe!

Here's what Marty found when she came home from school.

"Jason Giraffe saved your baby sister," Marty's mother said.

"Every kid who has a baby sister in a city apartment should have a giraffe," Marty said, hugging Jason.

UP FOR GRABS–
A
GIRAFFE STORY

(pages 77-80)

1. Why did the voice Marty heard seem to travel a long way?

2. Why did Marty's mom think her lamp looked funny?

3. What did Jason do after Marty's sister began to topple out of the window?

4. Reword these phrases to show possession.
   the neck of Jason
   the spots on a giraffe

5. Find two possessives in the story that use the same form as Marty's lamp.

1. The voice was a giraffe's, and giraffes are much taller than girls.
2. She thought Marty had painted spots on it.
3. He stuck his head out the window and caught the baby by the seat of her diaper.
4. Jason's neck, giraffe's spots
5. Jason's request, Marty's room, Marty's mother, Marty's baby sister

ANSWERS

HE'S NUTS ABOUT SQUIRRELS

There's more to working than just making money, and Richard Feeney is one man who could tell you why. For twenty-four years he worked at a job for which he never earned a penny. And now, no one is doing that job because Richard has retired.

The job was Official White House Squirrel Feeder. Richard got the job when he was five years old and kept it until he was twenty-nine.

In 1949, President Harry S. Truman, answering a great need, named Richard Feeney to the post of Official White House Squirrel Feeder.

As a child, just after World War II, Richard often played in Washington, D.C.'s Lafayette Park. It was a lovely park, and he loved to feed the squirrels that lived there. Richard didn't spare the peanuts, and the squirrels in Lafayette Park became fatter and fatter with each helping.

At that time Richard's father, Captain Joseph
Feeney, worked across the street from Lafayette
Park. Captain Feeney worked in the White House as
an assistant to the President, Harry S. Truman.

Often, the young boy waited for his father, and
sometimes he got a chance that not many people
ever get. He spoke to the President of the United
States of America!

Once, when young Richard was sitting on the
President's lap, he said, "Mr. President, you may not
have noticed, but the squirrels across the street in
Lafayette Park are much fatter and healthier
than those that live right here on the White House
grounds."

Being a truly great President, Mr. Truman made an instant decision. He created the job of Official White House Squirrel Feeder. Then he named Richard to the post.

When newspaper reporters heard about the new post, they didn't waste a minute's time. They asked President Truman about the new position at the White House.

The President said, "The job will have no time limit. It will be Richard's for as long as he wishes to perform its duties. There will be no salary, but I am sure the job will be well done."

The job must have been perfect for a young boy growing up in Washington, D.C. What fun it must have been, and how proud Richard must have been to do it!

As the years passed and Richard Feeney grew to manhood, it wasn't as easy to find the time to feed the many squirrels that lived within the White House grounds. Eventually, Richard got a job at the White House.

Now that Richard can no longer give his attention to the task of squirrel feeding, no one is doing that special job.

Maybe you can convince the President that he needs you. Are you ready to go to work?

HE'S NUTS ABOUT SQUIRRELS

(pages 82-85)

1. What chance did Richard get that not many people ever get?

2. How many years did Richard keep the job?

3. Why did the White House need a Squirrel Feeder?

4. Pick the sentence that shows possession.
   - Richard's going to work.
   - They didn't waste time.
   - He was on the President's lap.

5. Find two possessives on the second page of the story.

ANSWERS

1. He spoke to the President of the United States.
2. 24
3. The White House squirrels needed to be fatter and healthier.
4. He was on the President's lap.
5. Richard's, President's

WHAT'S FOR DINNER, DAD?

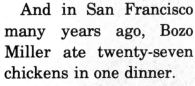

Mike Wright once ate eighteen hot dogs in five minutes. That's some eating! A man named Joe ate 437 clams in ten minutes.

And in San Francisco many years ago, Bozo Miller ate twenty-seven chickens in one dinner.

If you're a hamburger eater, try this on for size: eighty-three hamburgers. In 1973, one man ate eighty-three hamburgers in two-and-a-half hours. That's right! His name was Matern.

Structural Analysis 18

A student once ate twenty doughnuts in fifteen minutes. That's more than one per minute. Whose belly ached?

For *long* eating you have to go to spaghetti to find the champ. One person downed over two hundred and sixty-two yards of spaghetti—that's almost as long as three football fields.

Do you remember Bozo Miller's chicken dinner? He's back again. He ate 324 ravioli in one meal.

Ravioli are like blintzes. A blintz is like a crepe. A crepe is like an eggroll. An eggroll is like a taco. Around here, we call it a stuffed pancake.

While some people eat a lot, others eat nothing. Many years ago, some Irishmen in prison went on a hunger strike. They drank a little water each day. Eight of them lasted ninety-four days—that's over three months—without eating.

But someone in Scotland lived on water, tea, coffee, soda water and vitamins for 382 days. That's over a year! Can you imagine starting off weighing 472 pounds and ending up weighing 178 pounds? That's what happened. How much of a weight loss is that?

We call that fasting. Don't you try it.

The largest hamburger on record was a two-hundred-and-thirty–pounder.

And the largest omelet weighed 1,234 pounds and was made from 5,600 eggs. A lot of hens worked hard to make that omelet succeed.

Do you like pizza? Someone in Chicago once made a one thousand-pound pizza. It was 346 square feet and twenty-one feet across. That's almost as big as your classroom.

But the biggest feat of all takes place in the desert every now and then. At some Arab wedding feasts the people cook eggs. The eggs are stuffed into fish, the fish are stuffed into cooked chickens, the chickens are stuffed into roasted sheep and the sheep are stuffed into roasted camels.

Give the recipe to your mom and dad.

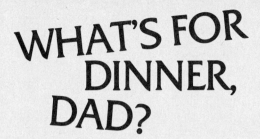

WHAT'S FOR DINNER, DAD?

(pages 87-90)

1. What is a blintz?

2. How much did the pizza made in Chicago weigh?

3. At some Arab wedding feasts, what do the people do before they stuff the sheep into the camels?

4. Which sentence contains a possessive?
   - That's right.
   - It was Bozo Miller's chicken dinner.
   - Don't you try it.

5. Which sentence contains a possessive?
   - Joe's hot dogs are hot.
   - Joe's eating hot dogs.

ANSWERS